I0202406

The *Art* of
BEING

8 WAYS TO OPTIMIZE YOUR PRESENCE & ESSENCE FOR POSITIVE IMPACT

BOOK 1 OF 8

SUSAN YOUNG

Susan YOUNG

Copyright @ 2017 by Susan Young. All rights reserved.

Thank you for buying an authorized edition of this book and for complying with copyright laws.

You are respectfully entrusted to not reproduce, scan, distribute, transmit or record any part herein without prior permission, with the exception of brief quotations embodied in critical reviews and certain other noncommercial uses permitted by copyright law.

This publication contains material for educational purposes only. The author and publisher have made every effort to ensure that the information in this book was correct at press time and do not assume and hereby disclaim any liability to any party for any loss, damage, or disruption caused by errors and omissions.

Library of Congress-in-Publication-Data: 2017912674
Young, Susan
The Art of Being: 8 Ways to Optimize Your Presence & Essence for Positive Impact, by Susan Young

Published by *ReNew You Ventures*
Editing by Elizabeth Dixon
Co-Editing by Judy Dippel, www.JLDWrites.com
Book Design by Kendra Cagle, www.5LakesDesign.com
Back Cover Photography by Rhonda Schaefer, www.RhondaClicks.com

ISBN-10: 978-0-9985561-2-3

To learn more about Author, Speaker Susan Young, explore her other resources, or hire her to speak for your live events, please visit:
www.SusanSpeaks.com

Contents

THE ART OF **BEING**

First & Foremost
Welcome to The Art of Being

The book you now hold in your hands began as a small chapter in a small e-book over five years ago. It was originally part of a gift I gave away for free as a thank you for visiting my website www.SusanSpeaks.com.

Over the course of a few years, my little e-book grew and evolved as I did. As I continued to speak, train, observe, research, interview, and enrich the manuscript, the content continued to grow and grow.

When the main book, *The Art of First Impressions for Positive Impact*, was finally finished, it was almost 100,000 words and over 400 pages! With 8 content-rich chapters that could make complete stand-alone topics, I decided to showcase each one and give it its own book!

In your busy life with everything vying for your attention, I wanted to make it easy for you to enjoy this valuable content in whatever form works best for you. Not only will this book and its happy counterparts be available in print, but also on Kindle.

So, whether you read the main book, one of the 8 small books, or all nine, these valuable lessons are timeless, true, and ready for you.

In this **Book 1 of 8, *The Art of Being***, you will learn 8 ways to optimize your presence and your essence to make a positive impact. However, let's first discuss the big picture.

Introduction to
The Art of First Impressions

Universally, what do most people want? Think about it. How about you . . . what do YOU want? To make new friends? Build social confidence? Have more fun? Be a stronger leader? Expand your influence? Get the job of your dreams? Grow your business? Nurture your network? Be your best self? Find happiness and fulfillment while engaging others? The list is long and unique to each of us.

You may ask, "Why is a first impression so important?" Because these brief seconds can be the make-or-break, live-or-die, or yes-or-no basis for building rapport, earning trust, winning friends, or making the sale. These "seconds" often determine your success in business and in life. What impresses you when you meet someone new?

Like it or not, your life—what works well and what doesn't—is largely the result of the first impressions you have created along the way.

❝ With every new encounter, impressions are made and opinions are formed in only a matter of seconds. The instant imprint you make on someone can impact them, and you, for a lifetime. ❞

Throughout your life, thousands of people will cross your path. Some you will remember fondly. Some you will remember negatively. Others will slip by unnoticed, perhaps because they were neutral, unengaged or, quite frankly, unimpressive. What can you do, beginning TODAY, to be the one who makes your mark and leaves others in awe? *The Art of First Impressions for Positive Impact* will show you how.

Do You Want to . . .

- Make new friends?
- Be heard above the noise?
- Feel accepted, included, and well-received?
- Make a positive and memorable impression?
- Be a part of something larger than yourself?
- Improve your self-esteem and self-image?
- Feel more socially courageous and confident?
- Approach new people with comfort and ease?
- Inspire, motivate, and encourage others?
- Have influence and inspire your team?
- Stretch beyond your comfort zone to create a daring adventure or experience?
- Stand up, stand out, and be well remembered?

Whether a first impression is made by a mere glance, a warm smile, a visit to your website, your poise and speech, or a formal introduction, it sets the stage for your relationships, personally and professionally. Regardless of the venue, you can increase your opportunities and improve your outcomes by making these opening moments matter. Applying these skills will ensure a positive experience to help you . . . Shine Bright and Stand Apart from the Crowd!

The Art of First Impressions for Positive Impact has the tools to help you prevent and avoid social mishaps, lost business, rejection, low self-esteem, failure, career complacency, and lifelong frustration. These principles and practices are enduring. Knowing how to make a great first impression will enable you to achieve your goals more easily and live out your hopes and dreams to become a happier, more content you.

8x8 Will Make You Great!

In each of the 8 Parts, you will discover 8 Arts filled with game-changing concepts that you can apply right away—beginning today! Seek to develop mastery in the . . .

1. *The Art of Being*
2. *The Art of Preparation*
3. *The Art of Body Language*
4. *The Art of Action*
5. *The Art of Communication*
6. *The Art of Connection*
7. *The Art of a Lasting Positive Impression*
8. *The Art of Nurturing Your Network*

Whether you adopt one over-arching principle or sixty-four specific techniques, everything comes together for good to make you more aware, better prepared, and empowered on your journey. The big book and all 8 of the small ones are formatted in bite-sized pieces so that no matter where you turn, you will find valuable tips and tools which you can read quickly to implement in your life immediately.

If you enjoy the content you receive in *The Art of Being*, be sure to visit Amazon.com to acquire the entire collection. In the meantime, let the transformation begin . . .

The Art of BEING

Attitude. Personality. Mindset. Spirit. Essence. Perspective. Regardless of how you define your state of being, your mental, intellectual, emotional, and spiritual approaches are the basis for your existence and how you experience life.

Your way of being impacts your happiness and outcomes—the wisdom of your choices, your confidence and courage, your self-esteem, how you are perceived and received by others, and the quality of your relationships. The more positively centered and grounded you are in your authentic being, the more people may be drawn to you.

The Art of Being lays the foundation for this entire book, as well as your first impressions, because if you get this part wrong not much else matters. All other efforts may be diminished or wasted. Someone who is being gracious, kind, and passionate is more likely to achieve what they want in life than someone who is being petty, cruel, or resistant. Your way of being sets the tone for how people relate to you, behave toward you, and engage. How is it working for you?

Becoming the person you want to be draws from being your best and doing your best as you allow your personality, passions, and purpose to shine through.

The Art of Being encompasses . . .

1. *Authenticity*
2. *Personal Integrity*
3. *Passion*
4. *Love & Generosity*
5. *Healthy Self-Esteem*
6. *Dignity & Grace*
7. *Charisma & Charm*
8. *Confidence & Command*

1. AUTHENTICITY

"Be yourself. Everyone else is already taken."
—Oscar Wilde

Being authentic is key to living a happy life and enjoying healthy relationships. I list authenticity first because if we miss this vital component of our unique way of being, everything else in this book becomes irrelevant.

ASK YOURSELF: Are you being real? When people meet you, are you straight up and natural—the real deal? If you are, then you will appreciate what it means to approach life always being YOU.

Standing in your personal truth enables you to transcend social layers of happenstance and get to the heart of matters—revealing what is raw and real.

Your goal, then, is to never be anything less than real or to clone yourself from another. Why would you be anything other than your unique and best self?

---

66 *Life's most amazing moments between people are built on trust, communication, acceptance, and love.* 99

As we observe and experience varying degrees of difficulty, negativity, loss, hurt, anxiety, and fear in life, we yearn for the reassurance that our relationships are safe. The days of the pushy salesmen and self-serving narcissists are over. That type of behavior quickly alienates and pushes people away because it offends and can't be trusted.

People must believe that you are real and are who you say you are, otherwise they will not want to do business with you, much less make the effort to move forward in starting and building a relationship.

When I meet someone who is truly genuine, I am drawn to their personality and find them easier to approach, engage, and interact with. I know that what I see is what I get. They have no hint of false pretense, nor do I worry about hidden agendas.

Authentic people are instantly more likable and trustworthy, which makes building rapport with them a pleasure. In their presence, we feel accepted for who we are without judgment or criticism. We crave real people and are delighted when we find them.

My dear friend Marnie Tate once shared, "An aura of authenticity is one of the finest qualities that a person can project. When I meet these sincere people and they look me in the eye—they have me."

Own Your Truths

"If you are your authentic self, you have no competition."
—Scott Stratten

Own your truths—all of them. Be honest. Be genuine. Be straight forward. Be refreshing! We gravitate towards such people, don't we? Allow your natural personality to shine through without pretending to be someone you're not, or you may be stuck with that label forever. Walking in alignment with your integrity will help keep you on the right track.

There is a reason that the words **natural, wholesome,** and **organic** resonate throughout our culture today. Aim to be natural and truly who you are one-hundred percent of the time.

We've all met people who are beautiful on the outside, however, when they open their mouths to speak, they have nothing of substance to contribute. And other times we meet folks who appear rather plain, yet when they speak from a heart of service, love, compassion, and wisdom, they instantly become respected favorites.

Authenticity is the litmus test for the honesty, transparency, and trust which are necessary for healthy relationships. You have met phonies—fake people who appear plastic and put on airs trying to impress other people. The person they present to the world is not the person who resides inside.

My friend Tina Hallis, Ph.D. (ThePositiveEdge.org) is a professional speaker who specializes in positivity in the workplace. One day after presenting her "Positive Psychology" workshop, an audience participant approached and asked her, "What about authenticity?

Sometimes I don't feel like being positive. What if I feel authentically mad, bad, or negative? Is that okay?"

Tina responded, "Of course it is okay! You need to honor where you are and it is not always about being happy. Your negative feelings are there for a reason, too."

Authenticity respects the ebb and flow between positive and negative. The people who really know you will understand that you are not always going to be in a happy place and an occasional bad mood is acceptable. By authentically sharing when things aren't right you allow the people you care about to offer the support you may need.

The Challenge for the People Pleaser

"Always be a first-rate version of yourself and not a second-rate version of someone else."

—Judy Garland

The challenge of being authentic for people pleasers is that we *really* want people to like and accept us. Being vulnerable, however, requires that we come to terms with the fact that not everyone is going to like us, and that it is okay. Not everyone needs to like us.

ASK YOURSELF: Do you really want people to like you for something that you're not? It takes a lot of energy to pretend to be someone else for the sake of pleasing others.

Teenagers especially go through this when they are trying to be accepted and fit in. As a lifetime people pleaser, I remember trying to mold myself into the person I thought other people wanted me to be—all for the sake of being liked and accepted. As a young girl, I allowed my self-esteem to be determined by others' opinions, and I devoted incredible energy tuning in to how everyone else felt. I wanted to win them over to the "Susan Fan Club," and when I failed, I was devastated.

Why did I think that the mask was a better portrayal than my authentic self? We can get hidden under layers of illusion, can't we?

I love to make people happy, choose to be positive, and usually have a joyful heart. Do you? While you would think my energy, enthusiasm, and passion would be great virtues, it annoys the hell out of some folks. I especially irritate negative, cynical spirit suckers who may think my eternal optimism is unrealistic and insincere. Oh well. I don't want to shut down and stop being happy to accommodate someone else. I've gotten to a point in life to understand that not everyone is going to like me. After all, I don't always like everyone either. That's life!

After I hit fifty, a friend of mine said, "Susan, this a great place to be because everything is either a "Hell yeah!" or a "Hell no!" I said, "You're right! You really can say no without regrets." Being my authentic self frees me to live out my priorities. I feel the relief. I don't waste time any longer saying yes to someone else's priorities just to receive their accolades and acceptance.

Additionally, being authentic means accepting other people for who they are in their own individuality.

---

66 *Authenticity isn't just about saying "this is who I am"—it is also about being flexible enough to recognize and appreciate the uniqueness in others—honoring the mutual respect for being authentic and true.* 99

Embracing Imperfection

"I know of nothing more valuable, when it comes to the all-important virtue of authenticity, than simply being who you are."

—Charles R. Swindoll

I am a recovering perfectionist, and like all in recovery, I do better some days than others! I have a friend who strives for perfection in all things. I have no idea how she does it. She always looks amazing. She is the whole package! Regardless of whether she is exercising, at the grocery store, or sweating in the sun at her child's ball game, she looks 'all together.' Being so darned perfect all the time makes a lot of people feel uncomfortable. They think she's wearing a mask and they don't think she is authentic, real. Even though she is genuinely very nice, they are intimidated by her need for personal perfection.

ASK YOURSELF: Do you generally feel uncomfortable around people whom you perceive to be perfect? Is there really such a thing as the perfect person? The perfect weight? The perfect shade of skin? Of course not! Our flaws are often what differentiate us from each other, and no person is perfect.

Brené Brown, Ph.D. is a respected thought leader who teaches the power of vulnerability and authenticity, bringing deeper understanding to our inner shame. If you have never seen her TED Talks, do yourself a favor and listen to her meaningful messages today. She gives everyone permission to simply be themselves. She quickly earns trust, respect, and affection through her own wholesome sincerity and transparent imperfections.

Dr. Brown shares, "Authenticity is the daily practice of letting go of who we think we are supposed to be embracing who we are." Why are we so critical of ourselves? We would all endure a lot less suffering if we would simply love and accept ourselves in all our imperfections.

In their book, *Forget Perfect!* authors Lisa Earle McLeod and Jo Ann Swan celebrate imperfection by providing a true and likely scenario. Imagine that you have just woken up. You have bad breath, messy hair, and are still in your pajamas with smeared make-up. You decide to sneak outside to grab your newspaper.

As you are tiptoeing quietly down your sidewalk, you realize that you have locked yourself out of your house.

Which neighbor will you go to go to ask for help? The one to the left, who is perfectly coifed without a hair out of place, has an immaculate yard, the perfect children, the perfect husband, the perfect figure, and more . . . *at least seemingly.* Or will you knock on the door of the neighbor to your right with four kids, dogs barking, a messy house, a sink full of dishes, and baby throw-up on her shoulder?

If you are like me, you would go to the neighbor whose life is real, authentic, messy, and in my opinion—*amazing*. Why? Because she is authentic. She is so secure in her beautifully imperfect self that she would welcome you with open arms, no judgment, and complete acceptance.

---

66 Authentic people are so comfortable in their own skins they make us more comfortable in our own. 99

Interestingly, being yourself allows others to be themselves. Even with crazy imperfections, being a bona fide genuine person is the best any of us can be—messy flaws and all!

As I mentioned earlier, moving to the Midwest from Florida was a major life change for me. The transition, however, was made easier by the authentic and friendly attitudes of the people who live here. "Midwest Nice" is true! I have repeatedly experienced their sincere kindness, caring, low-key attitude, and acceptance.

When my friend Jackie lived in a rich section of Atlanta, she felt pressured to wear the right shoes, drive the right car, sport the right hairstyle, and dress a certain way to fit in and be accepted. When she moved to Madison, she found that it didn't matter how she showed up. As long as she showed up as her real and authentic self she would be warmly embraced.

Admittedly, there will be times when you must interact on a superficial level and adjust your behavior to fit in, to go along to get along. Not everyone is always going to like you. What impresses one person may turn another away. To thine own self be true. Living in alignment with your true self enables you to cultivate transparency and unshakable authenticity.

2. Personal Integrity

"To give real service you must add something which cannot be bought or measured with money, and that is sincerity and integrity."

– Douglas Adams

Integrity is a most valued human quality. Your integrity is your personal code of honor which has the power to build your reputation or destroy it, establish credibility or crumble it—in one swift move. Your personal integrity, defined as being honest and having strong moral principles, communicates whether (or not) you can be trusted. Integrity, once tarnished, or broken, is hard to recover.

Think of the people whom you love, like, trust, and admire. Isn't their integrity the golden thread which elevates them to a higher standard in your eyes and in your heart? Being able to depend on a person's integrity lays a solid foundation for a relationship built on trust, both in business and in life.

Your Character Blueprint

My first career out of college was in real estate, where I specialized in new home construction. It was rewarding to help clients find their land, design their homes, monitor construction, and work to bring it all to completion. Being involved in the process from start to finish brought me great fulfillment as I watched their vision become their reality.

Their home blueprints always came in the same sequential order. The first page illustrated the new home's exterior, complete with roof lines, windows, siding, landscaping, and doors. The second page featured the floor plan's walls, and diagram specifics like the placement of cabinets, fireplaces, plumbing, appliances, and more. As we would progress to the third page, we would dig deeper into the electrical wiring to see what the interior walls would hold inside. Finally, on the last and final page, you would find the design for the foundation.

This last page was never fancy. As a matter of fact, it was rather plain, humble, and simple. The irony, however, is that the foundation was the most essential element in the entire construction process. Yet, the exterior **first impression** is how most would judge the value of the home—similar to what we do when meeting new people.

When a foundation is built following sound structural principles, with solid, high-quality materials, anything that is layered on top is more secure, durable, and resilient. However, if the foundation is poorly designed and constructed with low-quality materials, everything layered on top can easily come tumbling down and become worthless.

As with construction, your personal integrity is the firm foundation upon which you can build a strong character, rewarding life, and healthy relationships.

Building a Rock-Solid Foundation

For this Florida resident, hurricanes were a potential threat my entire life. When Hurricane Ivan hit the Gulf Coast in 2006, it devastated Northwest Florida. This treacherous hurricane stripped thousands of homes down to their foundations. Because of the chaos and destruction, the foundations were often all that remained.

This metaphor illustrates what happens in the human experience when our lives are ravaged by the storms of life. Through change and challenge, if our personal foundations are built with quality virtues of character and integrity, we are more resilient, healthy, and ultimately more impressive.

Throughout the history of mankind, the virtues embraced by humanity have remained true, unwavering, and consistent. While many may claim that these virtues are old-fashioned, they are essential materials for building a solid and worthwhile foundation for your life that will never go out of style:

- Integrity
- Honesty
- Diligence
- Charity
- Justice
- Courage
- Patience
- Kindness
- Humility
- Reverence
- Work ethic
- Compassion
- Persistence
- Wisdom
- Humanity
- Morality
- Decency
- Goodness

ASK YOURSELF: What do each of the words above really mean to you? Which ones are your strengths? Which ones might you need to improve upon? If more than one, work on one at a time, in order of personal priority.

The Illusion of External Appearances

Our modern-day society is often so consumed with external appearances that living a virtuous life may sound boring and dull. You know the ones! They are the people who invest all their focus, energy, and effort into how they look and what they own. While having a strong character foundation may not sell newspapers, increase TV ratings, or make a person famous, it's essential for building a life that is meaningful and matters.

When you take the high road to living a virtuous life, you are fortified by knowing that regardless of what life throws your way or what storms may rage, you are grounded in goodness. In this, you secure not only your own integrity, but you secure it in the eyes others.

Knowledge Without Integrity has No Value

"The greatness of a man is not in how much wealth he acquires, but in his integrity and his ability to affect those around him positively."

– Bob Marley

Have you ever known a person who was highly intelligent, yet their lack of character destroyed your impression of them? Even though they may have been accomplished, articulate, and knowledgeable, their words became impotent and irrelevant. It was hard to take their word at face value, wasn't it?

Years ago, I worked with a person who was incredibly bright, very industrious and creative—like a fox. He used the best (and the worst) of his talents to be a top producing salesman, but . . . there was a cost. He would do anything and everything it took to make the sale. He bent the truth, manipulated the facts, and told bold-faced lies.

Month after month, his selling success was evident. However, in the eyes of the people around him, he was failing at his game. He could not be trusted and we simply learned to keep him at arm's length so that we would not get burnt in the process. He created a dual reputation for talent and dishonesty. Making money and being prosperous is a wonderful place to be, but not at the expense of your ethics, integrity, and reputation. It is simply not worth it. It nixes any chance of creating trusted working relationships.

UN-Impressives

A lack of integrity shows up in unlimited ways, some of which include:

- Cheating
- Dishonesty
- Bold-faced lies
- Stealing credit
- Deceitfulness
- Fraudulent behavior
- Underhandedness
- Corruption
- Breaking promises
- Representing one thing and being another
- Pandering to what a person wants to hear even though you do not believe it yourself
- Stretching the truth to fit your story
- Exaggerating the facts in hopes to impress
- Manipulating others for your personal gain

ASK YOURSELF: Is there any way, as mentioned above, in which you are being UNimpressive? If you answer yes, make a fresh start today by choosing to avoid that behavior.

> *"Integrity is doing the right thing, even when no one is watching."*
> —C. S. Lewis

3. PASSION

"A person can succeed at almost anything for which they have unlimited enthusiasm."
—Charles M. Schwab

Desire. Enthusiasm. Purpose. Pleasure. Delight. Peace. Power. However you define passion, it is at the heart of your motivation. Feeling passion fuels your spirit and feeds your joy. It's a catalyst for action and provides you with the emotional stamina to stick with it, regardless of the obstacles. Every day should have threads of passionate pursuits within it.

What turns you on, tunes you in, and lights your fire? Think of the times in your life when you have been deeply passionate about something. Whether it is for your family, a cause, a person, an adventure, a hobby, a career, a love for music, or even going to the beach—your deep passion for it helps you tap into your unique personal power to live and love your life out loud.

When passion is lit, the fire permeates your being with the positive expectation that all is well and everything will turn out great.

To be truly satisfied that your life is well-lived, the object of your passion is something you feel you must *be, do,* or *have.* What lights your fire?

My friends Rolf and Monika have a passion for fine wines. Ron and Joy have a passion for boating. Kathy has a passion for painting. Daniel has a passion for staying fit. My mother has a passion for her flower gardens. I have a passion for speaking. As you see, it is not just about the object of your focus or desires—it is the compelling emotion, fulfillment, and intense enthusiasm that it engenders.

Passion Inspires Excellence

"Passion is the genesis of genius."
—Anthony Robbins

Are you impressed when you meet people who are filled with passion and conviction? Their energy is contagious and can make us all want "some of what they're having!" When a person exudes passion, it is evident that they love what they are doing. Their passion projects an aura of confidence and decisiveness.

Whether they are passionate about business, pets, paddle boarding, golf, or videography, when they share their passions, their fervor makes them all the more fascinating.

What are they doing that you would like to do too? How can you emulate their energy and enthusiasm? If their marriage is happy and passionate, ask "What can

I learn from them?" If they share ideas and exhibit expertise, ask "How can I take what I have learned from them and be the best at what I do?"

Passion inspires us to be to be better in our own pursuits and situations. We are motivated by people that share our passion and provide living evidence that it (whatever your passion) can be done.

Passion Fosters Participation

*"Passion is what you feel when you get
a glimpse of your potential."*
—Unknown

Do you want to gain buy-in for your ideas or win people to your way of thinking? Sharing your passion with others will not only enlighten them to your dedication and commitment, it can enable you to garner their participation, collaboration, cooperation, and endorsement.

Passion Empowers Persistence

I love the adage "Obstacles are what you see when you take your eyes off the prize." When we are deeply passionate about something, the obstacles or challenges are diminished by sheer will and desire. When you want something badly enough, it does not matter whether it is going to be easy. The passion will push you forward. When people are not passionate about their goals, everything is more of a struggle.

---

66 *Passion is the fire that gets us moving and keeps us motivated regardless of what roadblocks impede the way.* 99

I once served on the Board of Directors for a Boys and Girls Club. At the time, we were funding, planning, and building a new six-million-dollar facility. It was a major undertaking with continuous challenges. Our passion for serving children transcended the difficulties we were facing with fund-raising, permitting, groundbreaking, construction, and more. Passion kept our hope alive, and today the new center is a reality.

Alignment

"A great leader's courage to fulfill his vision comes from passion, not position."

—John Maxwell

When your passion is aligned with your purpose, you are unstoppable! It is in that zone of high octane congruence that you are turned on and "cooking with gas." Passionate people are great about discovering what lights their fire and going for it. They might be encouraged by others who share their passion, but they don't rely on others to tell them what they need to do or how they need to do it.

I once took a corporate position that was so completely disconnected from my passions, integrity, and dreams, that I became physically ill from the misalignment and developed an ulcer. Needless to say, I chose to leave. Thank God! Although this job would have given me a great income, my friend Julie McCarthy reminds me—**it is better to receive a paycheck of the heart.** When we hold true to our passions, we are authentic and living in alignment with our integrity and our passion-filled calling.

Passion gives you direction. It's an inner compass that links you to action. When you choose a career that is aligned with your passion, the work becomes irrelevant because the fulfillment outweighs everything.

As you can guess, one of my greatest passions in life is empowering others with tools to live their best lives. As a lifelong student of the motivational and self-improvement genre, my passion for speaking was ignited at the early age of twenty-two. The passion never wavered and finally, fifteen years later, I started my own company to speak professionally. It was the alignment of my passion that kept the embers burning because, believe me, the obstacles were many.

Working for a company may provide a more consistent and predictable income, however, I wouldn't enjoy the reward of motivating the masses and seeing lives changed for the better. I'm dedicated to living in alignment with my passion. It makes me remarkably happier in more ways than one.

Passion Can Ignite Your Business Success

"I have always found, in business development, that passion is the number one factor in making a good first impression. You can promise excellent service, great pricing, and flawless products, but none of that will be believed in your first meeting . . . unless you believe passionately in it yourself. Learn what makes you different than the other companies in your space— and show your passion."

—David Sears, Print Resource

I love the saying "If you're not passionate about your business, neither am I." As a national speaker, I work with companies who want to engage their customers, and it is common to see varying degrees of passion among their employees. When they lack passion, it is nearly impossible to deliver excellent customer service. Doesn't it make you less inclined to want to do business with them as well?

One interaction can make or break the experience—forever! When an employee, a team, or a company is passionate about their products and services, I am more inclined to bring them my business. Aren't you? It can't be taught to all, but people who deliver exceptional work, merely by relaying their passion through what they say and do in the workplace, are priceless.

A motivated workplace is key to getting the best out of your people. When employees are motivated and love what they do you will see higher productivity, less turnover, healthier communication, increased loyalty, and a happier environment. As the adage says, **you will never reach the peak of your potential unless you love what you are doing.** Put the right people in the right positions. Create the space for them to develop and deliver their strengths and talents. If you want to improve performance and productivity, set a vision that inspires and delights.

Passion Transcends Words

"Passion is energy. Feel the power that comes from focusing on what excites you."
—Oprah Winfrey

This speaks volumes! At the end of a transformational workshop I attended in Ft. Lauderdale, Florida, we were each asked to stand in front of the group, tell our story, and share how the lessons learned over the weekend had positively impacted our lives.

A young man from South America stood up and tried earnestly to explain, in broken English, what an extraordinary shift he had experienced. He was incredibly passionate, but we could not understand what he was trying to say. Without speaking in his native language, he struggled to express his depth of passion.

The workshop leader then asked him to speak his heart in Spanish. The passion with which he shared his feelings bordered on ecstasy. Even though we could not understand his words, we understood his heart and felt his extraordinary passion. We were all covered in goosebumps, and with tears in our eyes, gave him a standing ovation! Obviously, there's more than one way to communicate. Talk about first impressions!

Like all good things, if taken to the extreme, zeal can nullify or contradict a good intention. Is there a fine line between passion and being nuts? How can such a powerful emotion hinder or hurt us? Passion can go to the "dark side" when . . .

- It becomes addictive and elicits negative behaviors.
- Hyper-excitement begins to annoy some people.
- You get so riled up you spew spittle.
- Uncontrolled enthusiasm runs amok and becomes obnoxious.
- Force-feeding your passion onto others alienates people.
- Over-zealousness borders on obsession.
- It goes past the realm of reality—is not grounded in truth.
- It is one-sided and not mutual and awkwardness ensues.

What Happens When Passion Leaves You?

Life isn't always easy and can be wrought with chal-lenges. Have you ever lost your passion? Years ago, I was going through a very hard time in life, striving to adapt and flourish in times of crisis and chaos. I turned to a counselor for solutions and guidance. It felt like my passion had died and I did not know how to re-capture my joy to move past the pain. He said "Susan your joy has never left you. You simply have sensory blockages that have buried your joy. It is still a part of your being and remains intact." He was right. I simply needed to excavate it by being resilient, resolving the blockages, and healing. As soon as I did, the passion, and joy, burst forth.

We've all been there. What is blocking your joy? What is preventing you from living your passion? We've all been through pain and needed to be resilient to keep moving forward.

---

66 *Think about the things in life that elicit passion in you and make you happy.* 99

My cherished friend Marnie Tate recently pub-lished her first book, *A Passion for Living.* Through ag-ony, ecstasy, trials, and tribulations, Marnie overcame and moved through life's challenges with humor, pas-sion, and positive expectancy. She shares her story of how passion was the golden thread that wove her life together to be happy, successful, and fulfilled. Her passions are varied and she approaches them all with a profound gratitude for living and a zest for life. She inspires us all to live in that state of grace by living our passion. She writes, "With passionate intention, figure out what you love to do and look for a way to do it! Find the real joy in following your purpose and consider it a privilege to live this day. You will connect yourself to more opportunities than you ever thought possible."

Passion is Contagious

Passionate personalities are attractive and magnetic. In his book, *The Passion Centered Person*, Gary Zelesky shares, "When you follow your passion—or more accurately, when you turn it loose to run free, dragging you behind like a Great Dane owner barely holding onto the leash—you will create opportunity. People will come into your life attracted by your vision and excitement."

Do you have a dream or desire that is burning a hole in your soul? What provides warm satisfaction and brings you simple pleasure? Whether it's a hot cup of cappuccino on a cold winter morning, taking a walk with your dog, coaching your child's baseball team, making more sales, or planning your next vacation, it doesn't matter. Fan that flame. Feed its energy. It will make your life more fun and more rewarding. Your passion is contagious so learn it, love it, and live it.

4. $\mathcal{L}$OVE & $\mathcal{G}$ENEROSITY

"Everybody can be great . . . because anybody can serve. You don't have to have a college degree to serve. You don't have to make your subject and verb agree to serve. You only need a heart full of grace. A soul generated by love."

—Martin Luther King Jr.

It Starts with the Heart

Love is one of our most profound emotions and enduring qualities for living a life that matters. This feeling of warm personal attachment and deep affection is what connects, unifies, and binds our humanity. Approaching others with a loving heart enables you to be more caring, compassionate, and empathetic. What's not to love about that?

Do you genuinely love people? Or at least make an effort to *like* them? Your first impressions will be made easier and more successful when you **start with your heart.**

Love is the universal language that transcends countries, borders, barriers, and differences.

It's an expression and experience that we all understand. Yes, we know and learn love from our parents, children, mates, families, and friends. However, love extends far beyond the people whom we know and it makes us a part of something much greater than ourselves.

Love Is in the Air

Love is not only one of the greatest blessings in your personal life, but when it is extended professionally, the possibilities are endless.

Decades ago, Southwest Airlines understood that putting their heart into the center of their business would nurture loving and loyal relationships with customers for life. Because of their genuine love and caring for people, they have become one of the most profitable and successful airlines in aviation history. Their heart logo exemplifies their mission and is integrated throughout their branding. Southwest Airline's vision statement clearly communicates their intentions:

> *"We're putting our heart on our airplanes as a message to the world: We care deeply about our people and customers, and we push ourselves to always exceed their expectations of what an airline with low fares can offer.*
>
> *The Southwest spirit has always been perseverant, courageous, and caring. Our new look embodies that spirit, boldly proclaiming what sets us apart."*

Do you feel the love? Who wouldn't want to do business with a company like that? Their loving first impressions secure positive lasting impressions for loyalty, referrals, and repeat business. How can you integrate love into your vision, intentions, and actions? When you **start with your heart,** giving comes easily.

Reciprocity & the Joy of Giving

---

66 *When you graciously accept something from someone else, you are giving to them in return. By accepting their gift, you're allowing them to act upon what is in their heart.* 99

Begin asking how you may be of service and you will soon discover that the true gift is in your giving. When in doubt, give it out. Regardless of what is happening in your life, there is always someone else worse off that needs your help. Helping another person will instantly shift your energy. As you go from being self-absorbed to focusing on others, miracles seem to happen. And incredible impressions are made.

The best-selling book *The Go-Giver* has become a household name and launched a world-wide movement. Its authors Bob Burg and John David Mann encourage businesses and individuals to shift their focus from *getting* to *giving*. They share that "The principles of the "Go-Giver Way," affirm that when you come from a place of authenticity, are welcoming and open, and create value for others, you will touch lives and grow your network of meaningful relationships." The "Law of Reciprocity" is activated and everyone wins. It's important.

Doesn't it feel great when someone does something nice for you? Especially when you're not expecting it? The irony is that they are getting as much joy by giving as you are by receiving.

---

66 *It's simple. You enrich your life when you enrich the lives of others.* 99

For others to be generous requires that a person accept their generosity for the cycle to be completed. There are people who say "No, don't get me anything" or "Thank you anyway, but I will take care of it on my own," not realizing that they may be denying the other person's joy of giving.

If You Want to Get Rich in Life

When I was an undergraduate student in Florida State University's Business School, I didn't have a clue as to what I wanted to do with my life. I thought business school was a good idea because I wanted to make a lot of money to become financially secure. So, there I was, sitting in my first class on my first day of my junior year in "Real Estate Feasibility."

My professor, Dr. John Lewis, walked in and began by saying, "If you want to be rich, find out what people want and give it to them!" My thoughts flowed . . . *That's me! I want to be rich! What does everyone need? A house! What pays big commissions? Real estate. Cha-Ching, Bada-Bing!*

From his one comment, I decided to get my degree in marketing and real estate. When I graduated from college, I went straight into real estate and became a professional Realtor. For the next sixteen years, I enjoyed a multi-million-dollar producing real estate career in Tallahassee, Florida. It was made possible only by my putting my client's needs before my own and delivering dedicated service.

The epiphany came years later when I realized that when Dr. John Lewis said, "If you want to get rich in life, find out what people want and give it to them!" he was not talking about money. It had absolutely nothing to do with money. It was about service to others. So, what do people want?

――――――――――――――

❝ *You and I may have never met, but I already know so much of what you want: to be happy and feel valued. We want love, connection, respect, confidence, health, vitality, passion, kindness, and success.* **❞**

――――――――――――――

We all want these things. When you generously provide them for others, the universe will generously return them right back to you. When you come to life from a heart of service, you may be surprised by the blessings you will receive.

Many people, however, have never discovered the power generated from a heart of service. They show up to life projecting a right of entitlement in which their needs are their first priority and they will do whatever it takes to forward their own agenda without any concern for how it impacts others. This behavior pushes people away, creates barriers for trust and communication, and leaves a bad impression.

Networking as a Place to Give, Not Get

My friend Joe Sweeney is *The New York Times* Best Selling Author of the book *Networking is a Contact Sport*. He encourages readers to reframe how they approach networking. "Begin to see networking as a place to give, rather than to get." When you come from this mindset, you will receive more than you ever expected.

If you're always taking, you will inevitably experience resistance and struggle. Without realizing it, you may be creating a firewall that is blocking you from receiving exactly the things you most desire.

Have you ever been to a networking event where someone approaches and shoves their business card at you? They don't ask who you are, what you do, why you are there, or even try to find any common ground. They are so focused on self-promotion that your needs, interests, and services are irrelevant. What a major turn-off and bad first impression!

After reading Joe's book, I started testing a few of his ideas with business contacts and acquaintances. Instead of asking for a referral or asking when I might be able to come train their team, I would simply ask, "How may I be of service? What are the problems and challenges that you're experiencing that I might have a solution for?" It is a refreshing and different way to approach relationships, and people appreciate it. Don't know what to say? Simply ask the other person questions.

Isn't it a delight when a new acquaintance asks, "How may I help you? What can I do to help you on your journey? What type of referrals do you need for your business?" They make a much more positive impression and seal the deal when they take the time to follow up and deliver on the needs you share.

Serving Your Community

Another friend, Brian Haugen, exemplifies a heart of service. He has served, volunteered, and managed special projects in his community for years. From being an Army Green Beret in service to our country, to being the Destin, Florida Chamber of Commerce President, Brian brings a passion for helping others.

He says, "You can walk into a room and know instantly who the people are that are simply out for themselves. I have a lot of folks in my business who ask me about my keys to success. And I will say we are heavily involved in Chambers of Commerce. And it always floors them. 'Really? You have had success in your Chamber?' The reason that people don't have success is because they go there always expecting others to give them something."

Networking events need to be so much more than just a place to gather business cards. He served on a Chamber actively for years before he ever gained a prospect.

---

66 *If you can establish yourself in the community as a giver, those people with whom you associate yourself will extend your branding far beyond you.* 99

His service has been the most important principle to succeed in business. The impression he leaves, to those who barely know him and to those who know him well, is that of an authentic and generous person.

How May I Be of Service?

When I first met my friend Michelle Reddington, I was very impressed. She was the co-owner and publisher of BRAVA Magazine in Wisconsin. It was evident from the beginning of our new friendship that she comes to life with a heart of service. She's genuinely living in alignment with serving women. She empowers women through her popular magazine—providing style, substance, and education to help each woman become the best person she can be. Michelle is authentic, brilliant, charming, and engaging.

You know who the men and women are in your life that represent these fine qualities. Take a minute to think about and appreciate them. They make an instant and positive impression that makes you say, "Yes! I like that person. I would like to get to know them better!" Are you projecting this gracious heart of service?

Messengers of Hope

"I slept and I dreamed that life is all joy. I woke and I saw that life is all service. I served and I saw that service is joy."

—Kahlil Gibran

When I attended my first National Speakers Association convention in 2001, I was struck by the outrageously passionate, generous, and friendly people whom I met there. Their genuine positivity and enthusiasm made me feel like I had come home to the 'mother ship' for all that is good in this world. I intuitively knew I had found my people!

Imagine putting 2,000 motivational speakers and world-changers under one roof at the same time—it felt as if the entire building was levitating. I soon learned that the high vibration for positive energy was being fueled by something greater than ourselves—the Spirit of Cavett.

Seeing that I was a first- timer, complete strangers would approach me with a warm welcome and an earnest offer to help me succeed. No question was off limits and everyone would share their advice and guidance with unconditional generosity. I had never attended such an event before or since.

You see, NSA was founded in 1973 by a man named Cavett Robert. His vision for our organization was to create a place where professional speakers could come together to collaborate, exchange ideas, share best practices, refine their craft, encourage excellence, and learn from one another.

Mr. Robert once said, "a desire to help others is our most noble attribute; it gives immortal momentum to life and is our only certain path to heaven." He lived by example and encouraged speakers to create a bigger pie so that everyone could have a bigger slice. Now, over forty-four years later, our association continues to embody his spirit and servant's heart philosophy.

A few years ago, our brilliant member Simon T. Bailey (simontbailey.com) delivered an impactful and profound presentation on the main stage for an annual convention. He cited startling statistics for the number of meetings, conferences, summits, and events being held every year world-wide. He not only reaffirmed that our business is big enough for everyone to enjoy success, but that in our negative world today, messengers of hope are needed now more than ever.

Speakers, coaches, consultants, though-leaders, experts, and authors who dedicate their professional lives for the love of humanity and the betterment of society are making a positive difference in the lives of millions. These messengers of hope make our entire world a better place through their love and generosity.

"A candle loses nothing by lighting another candle."
—James Keller

5. HEALTHY SELF-ESTEEM

"You're always with yourself, so you might as well enjoy the company."
—Diane Von Furstenberg

There will never be another you! It's true. Did you notice that this chapter is entitled "Healthy Self-Esteem" not "High Self-Esteem?" There is a distinct difference that is worth noticing.

Being healthy, balanced, and positive is key to making a positive first impression. A **high self-esteem**, however, can quickly deteriorate into egotism, arrogance, and an over-confidence that can backfire and turn people off.

Your **healthy self-esteem** is one of the most significant and powerful drivers in your life. It drives your perceptions, attitudes, opinions, relationships, communications, and your decisions.

---

66 How you think and feel about yourself sets the tone for how other people feel about you too. When you feel great about you, personal qualities radiate that make you more attractive and compelling to others. 99

While developing a healthy self-esteem is a lifetime learning process, you can take daily steps to enjoy a confident sense of well-being.

When you have a healthy self-esteem, qualities such as likeability, confidence, trustworthiness, compassion, sense of humor, empathy, and optimism all serve to make you more interesting and successful. But unfortunately, we sometimes get in our own way . . .

Self-Talk & Your Inner Critic

"Low self-esteem is like driving through life with your hand-brake on."
—Maxwell Maltz

I can . . . I can't. How do you speak to yourself? Do you ever feel as though you have an angel on one shoulder and a devil on the other? And they continually argue over your self-worth, competence, and personal value? Which one usually wins the debate?

Your inner critic is that voice in your head that second-guesses your choices, doubts your abilities, judges your appearance, criticizes you at every turn, and tries to convince you that you are never good enough.

That voice is mean, unforgiving, punishing, and downright hurtful. When you allow it to run roughshod over your happiness and emotional well-being, it can wreak havoc on your peace of mind and leave you feeling anxious, fearful, and depleted.

This demoralizing self-talk leads to a self-destructive mindset, making everything in life more difficult. Not only that, how you feel about yourself oozes out of your pores and makes a bad impression on others.

We all can give in to our inner critic. I don't know about you, but I would never allow anyone to speak to me the way I speak to myself! I wouldn't be their friend! If you wouldn't want to hang out with someone who was constantly bashing you with a barrage of belittling insults, why would you allow them to live in your head?

Well, I have great news! You can take your power back and silence the criticism and lies NOW! How?

- Notice what your inner critic is saying, and issue a **cease and desist!** Regain control. Resist, and refuse to listen.
- Disrupt your thinking by saying, "Cancel! Cancel!" thereby interrupting the negative thought patterns. This not only has a psychological effect, but a physiological one, as well.
- Replace your negative mind chatter with positive affirmations and positive thinking.
- Take deliberate steps to retrain your brain and turn your inner critic into an enthusiastic, devoted fan.
- Become your own best friend—smile and say "I love you" to yourself occasionally.

> 66 *Focusing your energy on the things you don't like about yourself is self-sabotage and defeating. When you re-direct all that energy into a more positive direction, you will feel the shift instantly to improve your self-esteem and attitude.* 99

Brendon Burchard once wrote, "A life filled with silly social drama and gossip indicates that a person is disconnected from purpose and lacking meaningful goals. People on a path of purpose don't have time for drama." Isn't that the truth? The people we know who have healthy self-esteem don't waste their positive energy feeding the negativity of tearing down others, or themselves.

Self-respect

"Our self-respect tracks our choices. Every time we act in harmony with our authentic self and our heart, we earn our respect. It is that simple. Every choice matters."

—Dan Coppersmith

It is hard to earn the respect of others when you do not respect yourself. Others may find it difficult to enjoy your company if you do not enjoy your own.

Popularity does not equal respect. It is not only kids who will do what they think they must to fit in and be popular—adults do it too. Wouldn't you rather have the respect of your friends and colleagues than succumb to pressure to do and say things that are out of character in order to feel accepted? You can overcome this habit simply by learning to say "no."

Healthy self-esteem rests upon a strong foundation of core values and an inclination to act and speak in alignment with those values. Living in integrity with one's principles that are held in high regard engenders respect—both from others and self.

Imposter Syndrome

"To establish true self-esteem, we must concentrate on our successes and forget about the failures and the negatives in our lives."

—Denis Waitley

It is human nature for self-doubt to occasionally creep in and take up residence. It happens to even the most successful people among us. In the 1970's, social psychologists Dr. Pauline R. Clance and Suzanne A. Imes recognized that many high-achieving individuals were unable to internalize their accomplishments despite evidence to the contrary. Their observations led them to name this unique phenomenon "The Imposter Syndrome."

We all go through times of self-doubt, times when we may question our abilities and hope we can live up to the expectations of others.

Have you ever . . .

- Experienced fear that others might find out that you are not as smart, confident, or capable as you project yourself to be?
- Had feelings of phoniness?
- Felt like a fraud?
- Given credit for your success over to dumb luck or great timing?

What we often forget is that most everyone else has dealt with the same struggles and uncertainties. You get to pick your response when this doubt creeps in. Will you allow it to undermine your confidence, or instead, choose to look at it objectively?

With an objective eye, take an inventory of your successes and enlist the honest feedback of a trusted and respected mentor or peer. Chances are they see you in a better light than you see yourself! Remind yourself of the many victories you've achieved and build healthier self-esteem and perceptions on those.

Love, Accept, and Believe in Yourself

"You have been criticizing yourself for years, and it hasn't worked. Try approving of yourself and see what happens."

—Louise L. Hay

Be mindful to love and appreciate yourself and become your own champion. This healthy and loving relationship will be felt when people meet you. Bestselling author Louise Hay shares that a lack of self-acceptance is the cause of most of our suffering. You will be stuck with you for the rest of your life so learn to be your own best friend. Take a moment, look at yourself in the mirror, and say, "I love you." It feels awkward at first. Do it anyway. Begin a great friendship with YOU!

UN-Impressives

I once heard the phrase, "What you are speaks so loudly, I can't hear what you're saying." When a person has unhealthy self-esteem, it shows in the way they walk, talk, and behave. Even without meaning for it to, their low self-esteem is evident when they:

- Whine and complain.
- Bully others to exert power and control.
- Find humor at the expense of others.
- Criticize, condemn, and judge others.
- Reject compliments.
- Justify and defend their shortcomings.
- Make excuses and blame others for their problems.
- Overcompensate for their self-doubt by bragging or over sharing—or in contrast, always saying they're sorry.
- Emotionally withdraw.

- Underperform.
- Focus on the negatives.
- Gossip and disparage others to feel better about themselves.

There is a better way and you can begin today. Building a healthy self-esteem will foster a happier well-being and create more favorable results for life.

10 Ways to Build a Healthy Self-Esteem

1. Take care of yourself—mind, body, and spirit.
2. Use positive self-talk and affirmations.
3. Learn something new.
4. Surround yourself with positive people who bring out your best.
5. Be your own best friend.
6. Focus on what you want more of.
7. Learn from your mistakes and do things better next time.
8. Always do your best and the rest will take care of itself.
9. Set goals that give you purpose and direction.
10. Do something kind and considerate for others.

"Tell me how a person judges his or her self-esteem, and I will tell you how that person operates at work, in love, in sex, in parenting, in every important aspect of existence—and how high he or she is likely to rise. The reputation you have with yourself—your self-esteem—is the single most important factor for a fulfilling life."
—Nathaniel Branden

6. Dignity & Grace

"The ideal man bears the accidents of life with dignity and grace, making the best of circumstances."

—Aristotle

A book about first impressions would not be complete without discussing dignity and grace. Do you see them as a state of emotional and spiritual being or a physical projection of courage and class? Perhaps they describe both. The radiance of dignity and grace creates a profound elegance which exists whether anyone is watching or not.

Dignity

"Dignity does not consist in possessing honors, but in deserving them."

—Aristotle

Dignity brings a quiet smile as I think of my own mother. I'm sure you have someone that immediately comes to mind as well. It is that quiet strength which reflects one's deep honor and self-respect. Likened to "still waters run deep," a dignified person is able to call upon their wisdom and experience to discern a situation and expertly navigate it with grace. Grounded by healthy self-esteem and personal self-worth, this admirable character quality can inspire awe and reverence.

Dignity is an inherent value and human virtue which represents the best of mankind. When I asked Daniel what dignity meant to him, he shared, "Dignity is a gracious pride without narcissistic projection. It portrays a calm confidence and awareness regardless of the environment or circumstances."

Indeed. Think of the people whom you have known who have endured unspeakable hardship, heartbreaking loss, or great adversity. Perhaps you are one of them. In spite of the circumstance, a person who abides in dignity and grace will use the lessons learned as ballast for their ship as they sail through stormy waters—taking the wisdom gained from life and using it to anchor their confidence.

When Pride is on the Good Side

"There are two kinds of pride, both good and bad. 'Good pride' represents our dignity and self-respect. 'Bad pride' is the deadly sin of superiority that reeks of conceit and arrogance."

—John C. Maxwell

Arrogant pride has given the word "pride" a bad rap. When it is all about ego, conceit, and superiority, of course pride will be off-putting and make a bad impression. It can destroy trust and shatter teams. One who behaves that way probably doesn't feel proud when alone—there's something lacking.

One of my friends was a Realtor in a luxurious residential lakefront development in the South. The high-priced properties resulted in high-dollar commissions, creating lucrative opportunities for the agents. They had one particular agent who was the consistent top producer month after month. Unfortunately, with his remarkable success came great ego and pride. He became such an arrogant prima donna that he alienated the entire office and negatively affected morale, leaving the broker no choice but to ask for his resignation. Yes, pride can go to the dark side.

However, *gracious* pride is a powerful motivator and an exceptional quality. It drives a person to strive for excellence, keep promises, not give up, be more resilient, maintain optimism, and hold their head high while enduring challenge and change. *Gracious* pride is a wonderful quality when it is used for good; it brings out the best in you and encourages the best in others.

---

66 *Dignity is pride's barometer.* 99

Grace

Grace is a demeanor which comes naturally to some but more difficult for others. The good news is that with awareness and practice, even the most awkward people can learn how to be both fluid and purposeful in their bearing. A wonderful place to start is to seek role models who exemplify this way of being and try their style on for size.

I remember one such role model very well. Grace

Kelly was a beautiful American actress who fell in love with and married the Prince of Monaco in the 1950s. As a young child, I remember admiring her real-life fairy tale. Her name matched her countenance as she became an international role model of grace and dignity for the entire world to see. Her simple elegance and refinement defined her aura and her era. For you men, flash back to Cary Grant. He exemplified masculine grace.

Grace is also an attitude of generosity toward our fellow humans. We are not easily offended and do not look to judge and label others. With a spirit of graciousness we are amiable, benevolent, and charitable.

UN-Impressives

A loss of dignity and grace occurs when a person:

- Speaks ill of others.
- Behaves badly, irrationally, or inappropriately.
- Makes decisions which lack integrity, discretion, or self-respect.
- Boasts, brags, and broadcasts about how great they are.
- Compromises their virtue and their values, leading to shame and disgrace.
- Acts without considering the impact it has on others.
- Lowers their standards to a point of humiliation or flagrant disregard.

- Injures, cajoles, or interrupts others.
- Loses self-control.
- Is impaired by drugs, alcohol, anger, or ego.

How Do You Restore Dignity Once It Has Been Lost?

"Don't judge me by my past, I don't live there anymore."
—Unknown

People sometimes make mistakes, do stupid things, and lose their dignity in the process. Whether from intentional actions, carelessness, or outright arrogance, a loss of dignity teaches people how to perceive you—and that perception may be that you are goofy, foolish, or unwise.

Can a tarnished, undignified reputation be re-polished? Can trust be re-earned? Can you turn a poor first impression into a better one? Once lost, can dignity be restored? Perhaps. The following steps offer a start:

- Be honest with yourself through self-assessment and reflection.
- Accept complete responsibility for your actions.
- Address the problem and take the action necessary to solve and eliminate it.
- Apologize and make amends to the people you may have disappointed, hurt, or offended.
- Forgive yourself for your transgression.
- Change directions. No matter how far you go

down the wrong path, always turn back.
- Focus on the qualities that you love about yourself.
- The proof is in the pudding. Prove your dignity, integrity, grace, trustworthiness, dependability and more through your thoughts, words, deeds, and actions.
- Dignity is a lot easier to get back if you had it in the first place!

10 Ways to Exude Dignity & Grace

1. Stay humble.
2. Live in integrity.
3. Maintain calm composure.
4. Exercise tact and discretion.
5. Think before you speak.
6. Listen thoughtfully, respond appropriately.
7. Be in touch with your spirituality and how you view the world.
8. Treat others with respect and understanding.
9. Stand for justice, freedom, and honor.
10. Don't participate in gossip and people bashing.

Your level of dignity impacts everything in your life. It affects the quality of your internal world for how you see, feel, and think about yourself. It impacts the quality of your external world in your relationships, communications, and interactions. It impacts how you are perceived and received when making a first impression. Living as a role model in dignity encourages others to do the same.

"We need to give each other the space to grow, to be ourselves, to exercise our diversity. We need to give each other space so that we may both give and receive such beautiful things as ideas, openness, dignity, joy, healing, and inclusion."

—Max de Pree

7. CHARISMA & CHARM

"Charming people have the ability to make us feel as though we've known them forever—even if we've only just met them thirty minutes ago. They bring an easy sense of familiarity and intimacy that we don't often feel with other people especially with people we've only just met . . . but it feels so natural that we never think about it."

—DrNerdLove.com

Charisma and charm are endearing qualities which go hand in hand to make others feel "lighter, happier, and a little in love" when they are around you. People with this gift exude a delightful demeanor—an attractive likability that enwraps you in their warmth. When they are authentically engaged, their positive impressions create memorable moments and leave a lasting impact.

Physical beauty becomes irrelevant because their exuberance and engagement bring out the beauty in you. They seem to possess a heightened sensitivity to the feelings of others—delivering gentle manners, gracious compliments, and sincere interest.

Aren't you naturally drawn to those people who are genuinely glad to meet you and eager to hear your point of view? It is not simply in the words they speak—they show their interest both verbally and non-verbally. They emanate an essence of caring, love, and compassion towards the people they know, and generously extend their aura to the new people they encounter.

Their engaging manner is grounded in consideration as they seek to get along well with others. People who exhibit charisma and charm are also said to be alluring, bewitching, captivating, magnetic, fascinating, enchanting, and seductive.

What is their secret? How do they do it? Where did they learn how to be so pleasant and engaging? If charisma and charm are such valuable behaviors, why don't more people put into them practice for improving outcomes?

Nature or Nurture?

There are differing opinions as to whether charisma and charm are innate qualities which we are born with or learned personality styles. I believe it is a combination of both. Young children demonstrate a propensity for this enthusiasm. However, smart adults realize that they can get further in life when they develop these special traits.

My Grandma Lorene Cullison exemplified gracious hospitality and charm. As one of my most significant role models, she demonstrated to me at an early age that you will attract more bees with honey than vinegar and life is lovelier when you make others feel valued. She had an intuitive sense of harmony and her first instinct was to nurture and put others at ease. These lessons have undoubtedly helped me succeed in life and love—and in networking while forging new relationships and business. It can do the same for you.

18 Qualities of Charisma and Charm

Charisma (presence, poise, magnetism) and charm (enchantment, attraction, fascination) are behaviors which can be learned and practiced. Whether you adopt one new quality or ten, you can begin to embody and apply these qualities to positively grow the presence of character, your reputation, influence, and effect. People who exhibit these favorable characteristics tend to be:

1. Patient.
2. Respectful and fair.
3. Open-minded for new adventures.
4. Sincerely interested in others.
5. Engaging conversationalists.
6. Creative and curious.
7. Easily humored with an infectious laugh.
8. Joyful and happy in most situations.
9. Complimentary and look for positives.
10. Knowledgeable about how to use physical touch appropriately.
11. Able to admit their mistakes or make an apology.
12. Able to grow from failure and find gifts in the pain.
13. Action-oriented and self-motivated.

14. Kind and considerate without expecting a nything in return.
15. Able to refrain from judging and condemning others.
16. Willing to show vulnerability.
17. Able to remember names and small details.
18. Adaptable to change, people, and situations.

Prince Charming

The romantic Prince Charming archetype from fairy tales and folklore portrays a sense of heroism, good looks, good manners, and quiet courage. Fairness and justice for all! Not only can he make others swoon, but Prince Charming inspires courage, admiration, leadership, and confidence.

These people do exist and are a pleasure to know. Their keen communication skills are attentive to what you want, what you are thinking, saying, or not saying. They want to hear how you are and what you've been up to.

In his article, "The Charm of You," for *Oprah Magazine*, Peter Smith, writes, "At its best, highest form, charm is a show of generosity and moral goodness, an extension of the self toward others that permits them to shine. By helping others relax and unfold, charm allows you to shine too."

When Charisma & Charm Go to the Dark Side

"If you go around charming the socks off of people there are going to be a lot of cold feet!"

—Unknown

Is it possible to be too charming? Absolutely! When it is insincere and overzealous, it can badly backfire. Misused and abused by men or women, charm can destroy trust, ruin a reputation, be annoying, alienate others, and make a person generally unlikable. These offenders behave in a charming way only when they want something like money, sex, promotion, position, or personal gain. Crafty and conniving charmers, use their wiles for . . .

- Gaining an upper hand or an unfair advantage.
- Manipulating people, situations, and details in their favor.
- Hiding their agenda for a secondary gain.
- Using other people without concern, bother, or gratitude.
- Hiding their dishonest motives and intentions.
- Making up for a lack of integrity, confidence, and self-esteem.

The key is to keep charisma and charm positive and underpinned with sincere and good intentions. Psychology Today defines charisma as "the ability to attract, charm, and influence the people around you." While it may seem to be a mysterious, ineffable quality—charisma is enhanced and enriched by a person's attitude and confidence, their aims and optimism, expressive body language, and natural effervescence.

---

66 *Your charisma and charm can make your moments more memorable for amazing first impressions.* 99

---

8. CONFIDENCE & COMMAND

"With confidence, you can reach truly amazing heights; without confidence, even the simplest accomplishments are beyond your grasp."

—Jim Loehr

What do confidence and command look like when you see them? Moving one step past a healthy self-esteem, they project an air of authority, respect, and deliberate intention. Confidence is silent, cool, self-assurance. Developing a commanding presence is essential for leadership and a powerful impact.

There can be a fine line between being confident and cocky. True confidence is not something that can always be determined by a first impression. It may take a few interactions to detect whether a person is full of false bravado or if they are the "real McCoy."

Confidence and command earn this authority by accomplishing uncommon things which elevate one's expertise. "The best captains are not made on calm seas" is a relevant statement which recognizes that when a person has been in the trenches they have the experience to back up their command. Their prowess inspires faith in their abilities and affirms they can indeed "put their money where their mouth is." Their confidence gives those they lead the assurance that their words and their actions are reliable.

In our natural world, it is the strongest of the species that claim their space, seek out new territories, explore their surroundings, and learn how to survive and thrive. It is those same qualities that enable us to apply confidence and command to transcend the mediocre and achieve outstanding results.

Confidence in Communications

My friend Suzanne Gaddis, Ph.D. is an international speaker and the CEO of www.CommunicationsDoctor.com. Years ago, she worked as a communications trainer and consultant for an organization whose director had recently resigned. The assistant director was automatically moved into the open position. However, there was a problem. The new director had enormous talent and a rich education, BUT, she had no confidence. Despite her skills, her team saw her as weak. She did not exert the confidence and command needed to unify and lead her people. People who show weakness appear vulnerable and less decisive. Confidence, or lack thereof, significantly changes the dynamics of communication and the ability to lead.

Once the new director received communications coaching and became more confident in herself and her new position, she began to earn the trust and respect of her teams. As she began to exude confidence and command, her people took her more seriously in her new role, which enabled her to get the job done.

We tend to listen to the people who believe in their

own words as opposed to those who don't. When we feel their conviction, they earn our buy-in. Whereas, we lose confidence in those who speak from weakness or with little conviction. Even something as simple as ending a sentence with the tone of a question mark rather than a period can diminish a person's authority and credibility.

Low Self-Confidence

"Low self-confidence isn't a life sentence. Self-confidence can be learned, practiced, and mastered—just like any other skill. Once you master it, everything in your life will change for the better."
—Barrie Davenport

When you feel low self-confidence, it is usually the result of the negative thoughts your inner critic whispers in the darkness of your mind. When your inner critic undermines your confidence, inner conflict, anxiety, and agitation take over. It tells you that you are not good enough, smart enough, handsome enough, worthy enough, or basically just plain NOT enough. It takes a toll on your self-confidence, doesn't it?

As these thoughts repeatedly turn over, whatever you choose to tell yourself becomes a self-fulfilling prophecy. If your self-talk leans toward the negative, the continual bashing will become debilitating.

What to do? Notice when negativity spins in your head and disrupt it immediately before it has a chance to take hold and stick. Even the smartest and most successful of people will experience lower self-confidence occasionally, but the difference is that they deliberately shift out of it and refuse to stay there.

Qualities of Self-Confident People. They . .

- Inspire confidence in others; they would much rather build people up than tear them down.
- Are proud of their accomplishments, but can remain humble without bragging.
- Face their fears head-on and are willing to take risks.
- Know that obstacles are only temporary setbacks.
- Tend to be optimistic thinkers and focus on the positives.
- Respect and believe in themselves.
- Don't make their self-esteem, self-image, happiness, or self-confidence dependent on another person's approval, validation, or acceptance.
- Take the initiative to move forward in the direction of their dreams.
- Act calmly and rationally when thrown curve balls.
- Are mindful about spending their time, energy, and interests on things that truly matter.

Leveraging Learning Curves

Building confidence is an ongoing process and

something that can be accomplished over time. Just because you may not feel confident about doing something now does not mean you will not master it later with ease. As you jump new hurdles, you gain greater confidence. Confidence can be achieved like any other practiced skill.

The first time Susanne delivered a public presentation her knees knocked together. She fought back a gag reflex as she was trying to choke down her fear. She had never done it before and speaking was far beyond her comfort zone. She is now a highly sought after speaker who loves every moment on stage and continues to blossom in her craft.

---

66 *You will build confidence by continuing to put yourself into new and innovative situations where you can learn new skills, grow your education, test your strengths, and improve your abilities.* 99

Just because you don't know how to do something now does not mean you can't learn how to do it later. If you are lacking confidence in something, just keep trying and don't give up.

Yes, learning curves can be painful, exhausting, trying, scary, and intimidating. How did you learn to ride a bike? One pedal, one balance, one turn, and one step at a time.

Confidence is not a goal or a final ending point where you arrive and then stop once you reach it. Rather, it is the satisfaction and reward you achieve by stretching to, and beyond, the best of your abilities.

14 Ways to Project Confidence and Command

Building self-confidence is like building a muscle. Your confidence grows in response to your intensity of usage and the level of performance you require from it. If you don't use it, you may lose it. Stretch, flex, live, and build!

1. Think and act positively by focusing on the positives in yourself, other people, and situations.
2. Steer clear of negativity and set boundaries so that when people bring it on, you can engage your force-field to deflect their distracting energy.
3. Use your body language and posture to project confidence. Shift your physiology into a more powerful pose or position and your mindset will follow.
4. Make and maintain eye contact.
5. Speak slowly, articulately, clearly, and deliberately.

6. Dress confidently in clothes that make you feel great about yourself. When you look better you feel better.
7. Embrace change and practice flexibility. It will make you more agile in adapting to new people and situations.
8. Be prepared for all things that matter.
9. Set goals and create a clear sense of purpose and direction.
10. Get outside your comfort zone. Stretch beyond your norm and try new things.
11. Walk the talk and project confidence. If at first you don't feel confident, fake it until you make it.
12. Identify confident people whom you admire and respect and notice what they do differently to project such confidence. Learn by observing role models.
13. Practice positive and affirming self-talk.
14. Nurture a balanced perspective and don't "sweat the small stuff."

"It all boils down to how you present yourself. Do you "look the part?" Do you carry yourself with confidence? Do you ACT the part? Do you speak the part? If you can, then you are developing Command Presence, which will make your job a LOT easier."

—Chief Ronald Richards
Forest City Fire Department, Forest City, PA

8 WAYS TO **MASTER**
The Art of **BEING**

1. *Authenticity.* Be honest. Be genuine. Get raw and be real. Own your truth and let your natural personality shine through.

2. *Personal Integrity.* Integrity is a most worthy human value. Reinforce it. It is a solid foundation, built on honesty, morality, virtue, decency, and trustworthiness.

3. *Passion.* Passion is at the heart of your motivation. Let it fuel your spirit and feed your joy. It is your catalyst for courageous pursuits—and it will provide you the stamina to stick with it.

4. *Love & Generosity.* You enrich your life when you enrich the lives of others. The gift is in the giving—in your family, community, business, and network.

5. *Healthy Self-Esteem.* Being healthy, balanced, and positive is key to making a positive first impression. How you feel about yourself sets the tone for how other people feel about you too.

6. *Dignity & Grace.* Dignity is a quiet strength which reflects deep honor and self-respect. It is a gracious pride without narcissistic projection which portrays a calm awareness and generosity of spirit regardless of circumstances.

7. *Charisma & Charm.* These endearing qualities make others feel "lighter, happier, and a little in love" when they are around you. People with this gift exude a delightful demeanor—an attractive likability that enfolds you in their warmth.

8. *Confidence & Command.* Confidence is silent, humble self-assurance. Moving one step past a healthy self-esteem, confidence projects an air of authority, trust, and respect—a commanding, respected presence.

Afterword

BY SHEP HYKEN

Few things are more important to us than how we are perceived and received by others—personally and professionally. Since meeting new people will continue to be a significant part of your life experience, it pays to learn powerful, purposeful, and effective ways to improve your first impressions. That said, "You never have a second chance to make a first impression." It's not known who said it first, but it has been attributed to Oscar Wilde, Will Rogers, and even Yogi Berra. Whoever said it doesn't really matter. It's a catchy phrase. And, if you only meet a person once, it is valid. However, my belief is that you do have a second chance to make a first impression. Even a third—or one-hundredth—or more!

Yes, upon meeting someone you make a true first impression. Then in subsequent meetings or encounters, you make a first impression that sets the tone for whatever interaction is to follow. It may be a co-worker you see every day. A customer you see once a month. Or, a family member you come home to every night after work. Each time you have an interaction, you have the opportunity to make your first impression a positive lasting one—and it is under your control. And Susan will help you bring it full circle.

So, with all of the impressions we leave with people during our lifetime, it's worth our time to know our strengths and weaknesses. What better way to figure out what to do and how to do it, than through Susan Young's book, *The Art of First Impressions for Positive Impact.* She shines a light on what is important and influential for positive engagement and interaction. I sincerely believe her book could become standard training for businesses and organizations alike. And when utilized personally, readers will have the tools to transform the relationships in their lives for the better.

I met Susan almost twenty years ago when she attended her first National Speakers Association's convention in Dallas, Texas. The positive impression she made on me that very day continues to be the lasting impression which I enjoy, respect, and admire now. Since that first meeting, and each and every time I've met with her, she radiates with charisma and charm; always smiling, always positive and always dressed like a star. Her energy, positivity, authenticity, and love for people have been consistently genuine and heartfelt. She walks the talk with dignity and discretion—encouraging others to do the same. As a positive role model for making a great first impression, Susan is a living example of her topic.

As a customer service expert, I work with companies who want to build loyal relationships with their customers and employees. I believe that positive first impressions are indeed an art form that forms the basis for every relationship, business interaction, marketing brand, and customer service experience we have. These first and lasting impressions are crucial for winning the hearts and minds of your customers and have the power to make or break your success in life and business.

In *The Art of First Impressions for Positive Impact,* Susan brings together thirty years of knowledge and experience to help you identify, enrich, and deliver the everlasting elements for building healthy relationships. You have the power to make amazing first impressions by learning, practicing, and living the concepts Susan has provided for you, served on a silver platter, in this book, in wonderful detail.

—Shep Hyken

Customer Service Expert and *New York Times* and *Wall Street Journal* Bestselling Author of *The Amazement Revolution*

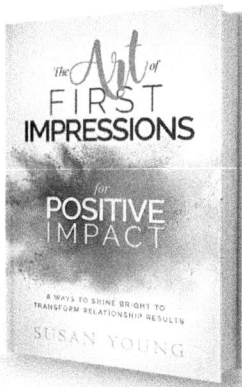

The Art of First Impressions for Positive Impact

8 Ways to Shine Bright to Transform Relationship Results

Now Available on Amazon

With every new encounter, impressions are being made. People will form an entire opinion about you— your company, your credibility, your personality, and your likability within a very few short seconds. These brief seconds can be the make-or-break, live-or-die basis for building rapport, earning trust, winning friends, or making the sale. These "seconds" often determine your success in business and in life.

Make these moments matter!

The Art of First Impressions for Positive Impact is your go-to guide to help you THRIVE in social settings and achieve the results you desire. Susan Young provides a rich and enduring resource to help you build engaging, valuable, and AUTHENTIC relationships forged in TRUST, COOPERATION, & RESPECT.

When the main book, *The Art of First Impressions for Positive Impact,* was finally finished, it was almost 100,00 words and over 400 pages! With 8 content-rich chapters that could make complete stand-alone topics, I decided to showcase each one and give it its own book! In your busy life with everything vying for your attention, I wanted to make it easy for you to enjoy this valuable content in whatever form worked best for you. Whether you read the main book, one of the 8 small books, or all nine, these valuable lessons are timeless, true, and ready for you. Please visit Amazon.com or SusanSpeaks.com to buy your copies today.

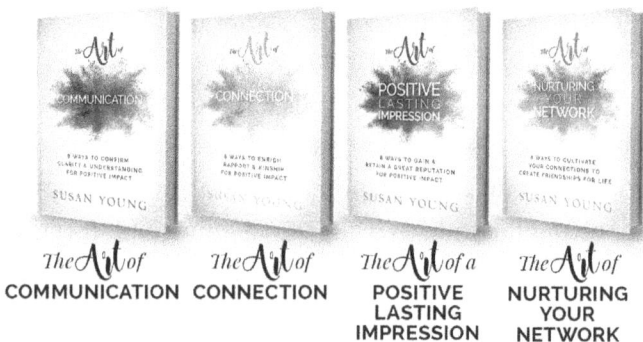

The Art of
PREPARATION

The Art of
BODY LANGUAGE

The Art of
ACTION

The Art of
COMMUNICATION

The Art of
CONNECTION

The Art of a
POSITIVE LASTING IMPRESSION

The Art of
NURTURING YOUR NETWORK

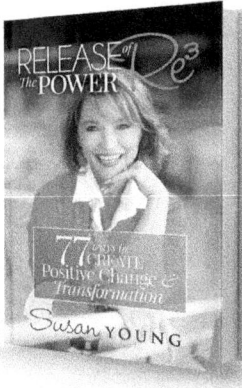

Release the Power of Re3

77 Ways to Create
Positive Change
& Transformation

Now Available on Amazon

Do you embrace change with optimism and resilience?
Or do you resist it with fear, denial, and frustration?
Are you at a loss for how to move past
adversity and challenge?
Would you like to create more positive
change in your life?

Then this book is for YOU! Change is't going anywhere and will continue to happen again, and again, with or without you, for or against you. That's life.

They why do some people strive and thrive, while others flop and flounder? You have the power to choose. In *Release the Power of Re³: 77 Ways to Create Positive Change & Transformation,* Susan Young shares her 3-Step Formula for harnessing the power of change, being exponentially resilient, and optimizing your outcomes in life and in business. Whether you hope to navigate change more successfully, create something brand new, or improve upon the past, Susan Young will help you make the right choices for the right changes.

About Susan Young

Susan runs the speaking and training firm, Susan Young International. She helps organizations leverage the power of change to improve positivity, engagement, and communications. Her keynotes and workshops empower people with tools to move from transition to transformation. She holds her Master's Degree in Human Performance Technology.

As a result of her work, people share that they are able to shift their mindsets, shed what is holding them back and reach a new level of potential to live a life they love. When she is not speaking to audiences across the country, training global sales teams, or motivating the masses, she enjoys dancing, biking, movies, and spending quality time with loved ones.

Susan is a grateful mother to her young adult twins, Nick and Ally and grandmother to Jace. Though a Florida native, she currently resides in Madison, Wisconsin with her true love Daniel Futch. She is a world traveler, scuba diver, interior designer, painter, avid reader, cyclist, and beach lover.

Please visit:
www.SusanSpeaks.com
to invite Susan to speak at your next event, join her community, or discover ways to move from transition to transformation.
We look forward to seeing you there!

Acknowledgements

Thank you . . .

To the man I love, my life-mate and partner Daniel Futch, for believing in me and providing me with the space, place, freedom, love, and commitment to help me live my dream.

To my brilliant sister and editor Elizabeth Dixon for helping me enrich my message by editing every word, concept, and idea. Your loving hands and profound guidance have made this book truly special. You have been incredibly patient and consistently loyal in the process—from its original inception five years ago to the final manuscript.

To my talented graphics designer and friend Kendra Cagle who helps me make an outrageously positive impact with her cutting-edge designs, colors, creativity, and innovation for my books and professional branding. (5LakesDesign.com)

To my content development editor and friend Judy Dippel (jldwrites.com) for helping me to expand my message and further enriching the importance of making a positive first impression.

To my wonderful family, including Ann Cullison, Marjorie Jane Chandley, Elizabeth Dixon, Jane Cullison Vosser, Christine Collins, Farrell Hendricks, and Carol Chandley Mondello.

To cherished friends Marnie Tate, Tina Hallis, Cheri Davis, Natalie Leon, Cheri Neal, Susanne Gaddis, Amy Tolbert, Laura Wells, Cindy Cooper, Nancy Fox, Jon & Esther Hemphill, Joy Todd, Monika Moritz Klam, Shep Hyken, Joe Anheier, Adrianne Machina, Ed Robinson, Julie McCarthy, Deborah Suzan, Michelle Reddington, Denise Pedersen, Peggy Libson and Julie Cleghorn.

Thank you to the fellow speakers and writers whom I have quoted for their inspired insights, words of wisdom, and dedication to be messengers of hope—life-changers and world-changers!

Please Leave a Review on Amazon

Thank you very much for reading *The Art of Being*. If you enjoyed reading it and sharing our journey together, please be so kind to post a short review on Amazon. Your support really does matter and I deeply appreciate your feedback. Thank you!

You are Invited to Visit Susan Young's Amazon Author Page at http://amzn.to/2vv8TcC

Let's Stay in Touch and Connect on Social Media

Susan_Speaks

susanyspeaks/

SusanYoungSpeaks

susanyoungmotivationalspeaker

+SusanYoungMotivationalSpeakerMadison

www.ingramcontent.com/pod-product-compliance
Lightning Source LLC
Chambersburg PA
CBHW071827020426
42331CB00007B/1631